A Feather of Moments
By Catherine Soto

ISBN: 9798365160750

Authors note:

Many of these poems were based on dreams I had or parts of poems that I would have to write down right away. I originally was planning on publishing this in 2021 but could never think of a title at the time and it didn't seem complete until now. I hope you enjoy and thank you for picking this up and giving it a chance.

This collection is dedicated to my grandpa who the last poem is about. Thank you for all that you taught me growing up and helping me to become the person I am today. I miss you, I love you and every time I find a feather I think of you.

If I told you "I love you"
What would you do?
Would you turn around, kiss me
Say "I love you too"
If I asked you to stay
What would you do?
Keep walking away like I know you want to
Or hold me and say "I'll never go away"
If this happens or that
Is it real or pretend?
The questions I wonder at night in my bed
Yet these what ifs don't matter
They don't matter at all
Because I ask these questions
I said these things
And now I smile and say
-Oh Well

As a kid all I wanted was an ice cream truck on my street
To be able to go outside and grab a sweet treat
This dream that so many kids have
The excitement they feel
The rare moment
The brief moment
The sound of that familiar tune
When I hear an ice cream truck on my street
I stop and smile and thank God for you
-A person I never met

Here we are
Standing in this parking lot just you and me
To the untrained eyed we might be lovers, or friends
The truth they don't see
Is that I just met you
Not in the physical sense of us being strangers and meeting for the first time
But today I learned some things
I learned that your favorite colors purple
Your eyes sparkle when you talk
About something that you love
You have a smile that can brighten anyone's day
It's the deep talks
The adventures
-What only a few people know

The talent shows
The stage that glows
Singing that one song by that one artist
Turns into the places we used to go
Stamped with laughter, the love and our friends
The bonfire pits
The bowling alley
Trying to hold on to this moment as long as I can
Fading into long drives
Getting lost in the sights of the moon and the night
These moments
These things
They're like
-memories on this town

Stay
Where you are is where I want to be
Here in this moment
This place we're at together
How did we end up in the middle of the dance floor?
You reach out your hand and spin me around
I never want this night to end
Feelings flooding my head
Butterflies and a calm sea
- You're my person

I’ll sing the melody
While you write the words
This collaboration we’re creating
Holds more meaning than we’ll ever know
This song is for
The one whose always anxious
The one who’s still finding themselves
The person mending a broken heart
And a happy couple too
Those who have lost someone
And those who have welcomed someone new
This one is for you
-one song a million meanings

You come to me in my sleep
I'm given an amazing opportunity to live my dreams
Thanks to you
Taking pictures at your concerts
Bonding with your friends
Behind the scenes
Filming vlogs and making memories
Holding hands at the state fair
Travels together and surprise parties
Living in this moment
Taking it all in
-Then I wake up

He smells of sandalwood and honey
His voice a bit raspy yet soothing
When he sings I'm in awe
I could listen to that song for hours
His laughter is my favorite sound
That smile, don't even get me started
It can light up a room
He's constantly glowing
But his eyes, blue yet green
All the colors in between
I say, "you have pretty eyes" and that makes him blush
He's adorable and handsome
Nerdy and kind
Deep talks over small talk
He's got amazing style
I vibe with his friends
-That LA Boy

Brown hair
Faded blue jeans
Nose ring, arm tattoos
He says that "We can't be just friends"
Snapback and a black t-shirt
Sitting on a roof top looking at the stars
Travel with me into space
Show me who you are
The boy who likes science, who knows about planets & the moon
Teach me how to be an astronaut just like you
Tell me your thoughts on Venus and Mars
Watch as the meteors put on a show
Your smile is radiant as you speak
Just like the sunrise we're about to see
-Nights like these are where I long to be

Neon lights
People screaming your name
But you’re looking at me
The girl of moonlight and embers
While you’re the guy of sunbeams and rain
They don’t know about us
Late night walks with deep talks
Movie nights & lots of cuddles
Midnight laughter
Time with our friends
As I raise my camera to take another picture
A smile forming on my lips
I sigh to myself and whisper
- “that’s my man”

Meet me where the sunflowers grow
That place where we used to go
Where we picked pumpkins in the crisp fall air
Jumping in piles of multicolored leaves
Laughter ringing all around
That was then, this is now
Different beds in different cities as you follow your dreams & I follow mine
Scheduled visits over spontaneous adventures
One day soon we'll look back at these memories the way we think of those sunflowers
And we'll smile as we sit on our couch in our place
Holding hands because we made it
We grew stronger & taller as we focused on the rays of light
-just like the sunflowers at that place we used to go

Little did we know that first meeting would lead to the next
A borrowed jacket because it was cold at that concert turns into
Spending time with your family, a place of safety and warmth
Spending time with my family, a place of comfort and hope
Joining your friend group full of laughter, adventures, creativity and love
Singing in the car and kissing in the rain
Dancing without a thought of if we look like dorks or not
Being with you is like a dream come true
-Little did we know what would come from a simple "hello"

Let’s run away to a faraway land
Full of pirates & fairies & princesses too
A place where witches cast spells and animals talk
There are epic battles, laughter and games
No two days are exactly the same
To Neverland with Peter Pan
Or thru the wardrobe we go
When I’m with you
-It feels like home

Your hand in mine, when they're intertwined
Everything's alright
Those chestnut eyes, the freckles on your nose
That 100-watt smile
Here in your arms nothing can hurt us
Our anxiety can't touch us when we're together
Your laughter fills me with serotonin
Watching the sunset with our friends around the bonfire
I look at you with my ocean eyes
You lean forward and softly kiss my forehead
Listening to the crackling fire, the waves on the shore & the sound of your heartbeat
This moment is serene
This moment is ours
- This is pure bliss, Happiness

If tomorrow our sky is no longer blue
I would still be holding on to you
The way your laughter brings a smile to my face
How you pull me closer when you sleep
Talks about life and what scares us the most
I know your favorite color and that one verse
From the song you would sing every time we drove in your car
Getting lost in the company
-of the ghost in this room

It was a Wednesday when I first met you
Under the light of the silver moon
Then Friday came and slipped away
Just like any other day
Saturday was full of blue skies, piggyback rides
And laughter that caused my sides to ache
On a Monday we had to say "See ya later" for a little while
As I went back home, and you stayed in LA
But on a Wednesday
- I was by your side again

You brought me roses
Shades of blues, purples, pinks
The colors of the sunset we watched on the beach
With our hands intertwined
You spun me around under twinkling lights
With laughter in our hearts
As our fingers interlocked for another pinky promise
The chill night air quickly brought us inside
- I borrowed your sweater and you laced your fingers through mine

The sailor met her on a Greyhound bus
She was a southern girl wearing a necklace with a B around her neck
He was a California boy raised on a farm
He introduced himself to the girl he called "Bonnie Lu"
Her name was actually "Bonnie Sue"
They talked for hours on that bus
When it was time to part ways, he asked "drop me a line when you get home?"
Bonnie Sue did just that
When she got home, she wrote "Dear Ralph" drew a line and signed her name
She returned to California three months later
They were married three months after that and again in the fall
The cowboy and the southern sweetheart had four kids and raised them in a modest house
Soon came a granddaughter
The cowboy took her under his wing from the beginning
He attached wood to a tree trunk in the backyard so she could have a thinking tree
Because she loved to get dirt on her clothes
She would dance on top of an old rusty hot tub deck until it had to be taken down
The grandpa taught his granddaughter about plants and showed her how to garden
She would always play with tadpoles and earth worms
Picking flowers and daydreaming
As the girl got older the grandpa cheered her on in soccer games, dance productions & talent shows
He taught her how to dream wild dreams but also work hard
She taught him how to be up for any adventure & to try and be more carefree
She was a cowboy just like him
Wild, free, and full of creativity
60 years the man was married to his beautiful sweetheart
Before the good Lord called him home
A love story for the ages
-And it all started on a Greyhound bus

Other works by author:

Jolted Desire - A short story
Love is… - A poetry Collection

You can find me on socials at:
Instagram: @dolphin_ocean_love
TikTok: @dolphin_ocean_love
Youtube: Life With Callyn

www.ingramcontent.com/pod-product-compliance
Lightning Source LLC
LaVergne TN
LVHW020547160826
845677LV00015B/4257

* 9 7 9 8 3 6 5 1 6 0 7 5 0 *